# GROUNDBREAKERS

# Michael Faraday

Ann Fullick

**www.heinemann.co.uk**
Visit our website to find out more information about **Heinemann Library** books.

To order:
☎ Phone 44 (0) 1865 888066
▤ Send a fax to 44 (0) 1865 314091
▯ Visit the Heinemann Bookshop at www.heinemann.co.uk to browse our catalogue and order online.

First published in Great Britain by Heinemann Library,
Halley Court, Jordan Hill, Oxford OX2 8EJ
a division of Reed Educational and Professional Publishing Ltd.
Heinemann is a registered trademark of Reed Educational & Professional Publishing Ltd.

OXFORD MELBOURNE AUCKLAND
JOHANNESBURG BLANTYRE GABORONE
IBADAN PORTSMOUTH (NH) USA CHICAGO

Designed by AMR
Originated by Ambassador Litho Ltd
Printed in Hong Kong/China

04 03 02 01 00
10 9 8 7 6 5 4 3 2 1

ISBN 0 431 10443 3

**British Library Cataloguing in Publication Data**
Fullick, Ann
  Michael Faraday. – (Groundbreakers)
  1.Faraday, Michael, 1791 – 1867– Juvenile literature
  2.Physicists – Great Britain – Biography – Juvenile literature
  I.Title
  530'.092

**Acknowledgements**
The Publishers would like to thank the following for permission to reproduce photographs:
BBC: p25; Bridgeman Art Library: pp4, 7, 21, 24, 28, 29, 35, 36, 37, 38, 43; Hulton Deutsch: p30; Mary Evans Picture Library: pp8, 10, 12, 16, 20, 22, 27, 32; Hulton Getty: pp9, 13, 18, 23, 31; Robert Harding Picture Library: pp15, 34, 40, Rob Francis p5; Oxford Scientific Films: p26; The Royal Mail: p42; Science Photo Library: pp11, 19, 33, 41, Jean-Loup Charmet p39, C D Winters p14; Science and Society Picture Library: pp17; Roger Scruton: p6.

Cover photograph reproduced with permission of Hulton Getty.

Every effort has been made to contact copyright holders of any material reproduced in this book. Any omissions will be rectified in subsequent printings if notice is given to the Publisher.

Any words appearing in the text in bold, **like this**, are explained in the glossary.

# Contents

# Changing times

In 1791 an unassuming couple in Newington, England, quietly celebrated the birth of their third child and second son. James and Margaret Faraday had only recently moved south from Yorkshire and times were hard. No one could have imagined the impact that their new baby, called Michael Faraday, was going to have on the world.

## A world of darkness

When Michael Faraday was born, King George III was on the throne of England. People still relied heavily on candles and oil lamps for their lighting, and on fires both for heating and for cooking. Steam power was used in industry but had not yet been harnessed as a method of transport and cars were undreamed of.

*From our modern homes and schools it is hard to imagine the lack of technology in the late 18th century.*

By the 18th century people were moving away from **alchemy** to a less mystical, more scientific examination of the world around them. Some interesting work was being done on electricity and magnetism, and scientists were beginning to question whether there was a link between the two. Scientific minds were becoming more rigorous and logical in the way that they worked. The time had come for scientists such as Humphry Davy, Michael Faraday and their contemporaries to flourish.

*Technology has moved a long way forward since the days of Michael Faraday, but power stations like this one still rely on the dynamo he invented.*

## A light shines out

By the end of Michael Faraday's brilliant life, electricity and magnetism had been more than linked – they had been yoked together in the form of a **dynamo** to produce electrical power at will. The dynamo is still, to this day, at the heart of electrical power generation (production) wherever it takes place, be it in a small wind **generator** in the developing world, or in a massive American power station. In this way and many others, Michael Faraday left an **indelible** footprint on the face of the earth.

# The blacksmith's son

*Michael Faraday's parents got to know each other as they walked across wonderful Yorkshire countryside like this.*

In 1756 Robert Faraday married Elizabeth Dean and together they moved into Clapham Wood Hall, the home of the Dean family. This was a small farm of about 19 hectares (46 acres) in Yorkshire, in the north of England, which produced barely enough food to support the Faraday family – by 1775 there were ten children! One son became an innkeeper, one a tailor, another a weaver. The third son, James, was **apprenticed** to a **blacksmith** as soon as he was old enough.

## James and Margaret

The Faraday family was similar to many others of the time, except that the Faradays were members of a small and exclusive religious group known as the **Sandemanians**. This limited their social life and their choice of people to marry, but James was lucky. His eldest brother Richard moved to a neighbouring village called Kirby Stephen, where he became a prosperous businessman and married Mary Hastwell, the daughter of another Sandemanian family he had met at the small local church. He suggested James set up a blacksmith shop close by at Outhgill, and introduced him to Mary's sister Margaret who worked as a servant at a nearby farm. James and Margaret regularly walked to church together and home again, and a relationship developed between them. They were married on 11 June 1786.

## A star is born

For the first year or two things went well. The **smithy** prospered and James and Margaret started a family. In 1787 they had a daughter, Elizabeth, and in 1788 Robert, their first son, was born.

*Michael Faraday grew up in a small mews, far removed from the elegance of this central London setting.*

But in 1789 England suffered a depression, as the dramatic events in Europe during the **French Revolution** brought trade between France and England to a halt. Worse, James Faraday's health began to fail – the strain of running his own smithy told on his strength. Travellers stopping to have their horses shoes renewed convinced him that he would do better in London. In 1791 the family left Yorkshire and moved into rented rooms in Newington, which was quite near to London. It was here that Michael Faraday was born, on 22 September 1791. Shortly afterwards, the family moved again, this time to Jacob's Well Mews in the capital itself.

# The apprentice boy

As a boy, Michael Faraday was happier playing marbles on the streets than working at school.

Michael Faraday's childhood seems to have been poor but happy. Times were hard because his father's health continued to be bad and so the family had little money coming in. In fact, in 1801, things were so difficult that Michael often had to survive for a whole week on a single loaf of bread! There were four children in the Faraday family. Michael got on well with Elizabeth and Robert, his older sister and brother, and adored his younger sister, Margaret, who was born in 1802.

## A genius at school?

Young Michael had very little formal schooling. He was far happier playing out on the streets.

The poverty of his childhood never seemed to affect Michael in later life, but the love and happy times he shared with his family, within the strict confines of their **Sandemanian** beliefs, were a lifelong source of strength to him. Sandemanians believed that every word of the Bible was true, and rejected material wealth and fame. They discouraged close friendships with anyone who was not part of their small community, so it was only on Sundays when, surrounded by fellow believers, Michael could truly relax and make friends.

### In Faraday's words:

Michael Faraday is said to have remarked: *'My education was of the most ordinary description, consisting of little more than the rudiments of reading, writing and arithmetic at common day-school. My hours out of school were passed at home or on the streets.'*

## The errand boy

When Michael Faraday was 13 he started work as an errand boy for Mr Riebau, a local bookseller and bookbinder. He delivered newspapers that Mr Riebau loaned to his customers, and then called back to collect them later! In between his journeys he must have spent some time in the shop, and began to develop a great love of books. He made a very good impression on his employer, who was a generous and kindly man. He realized that the Faraday family would never be able to afford the **apprenticeship** fees for Michael and, in 1805, offered to take him on as an **apprentice** bookbinder for nothing. These were happy times for Michael – he enjoyed his work and loved reading the books he was binding.

*Inspired by the science books found in Mr Riebau's bookshop, the young Faraday began to experiment with electrical machines. Here, Mr Riebau demonstrates one of the machines to a possible patron.*

*Attending lectures given by leading scientists of the day opened up a whole new world for Michael Faraday.*

Michael Faraday and his fellow **apprentices** had a very enjoyable time when they worked for Mr Riebau the bookbinder, but none of them followed him into the profession they were training for. Faraday became a great scientist and his two fellow apprentices became a comedian and a professional singer respectively! So there was good company and, for Faraday at least, a great deal of reading. A book called *Improvement of the Mind* was an inspiration to him, giving structure and method to his thoughts, and he also devoured science books and encyclopaedias.

## The City Philosophical Society

After reading some articles by a chemist called Mr James Tytler about his work on electricity, Faraday was captivated by the subject. Michael's brother, Robert, paid the shilling (5 pence) fee for him to attend some science lectures given by Mr John Tatum, who was a member of the **Royal Institution**. Tatum set up the City Philosophical Society at his home, to provide an opportunity for young men interested in science to meet, hear lectures and carry out experiments. There Faraday met a group of other like-minded young men and exchanged ideas and letters with them on the subjects of physics and chemistry.

## The Davy lectures

In 1812 Mr Dance, a customer of Mr Riebau and a member of the Royal Institution, was so impressed with some of Faraday's chemistry work that he gave the young man tickets for a series of four lectures to be given at the Institution by Sir Humphry Davy, the greatest scientist of the day. Captivated, Faraday made detailed lecture notes as he listened. He later illustrated and bound these notes that were to stand him in very good stead in the future.

In 1812, after seven years, Faraday's **apprenticeship** was over – he was a qualified bookbinder – and he could no longer stay at Mr Riebau's bookshop. He got a job with another bookbinder, a Frenchman called De La Roche, who was known for his short temper. Although Michael was now earning some money and could help to support the family, he was very unhappy with his work. He became more and more determined to leave bookbinding and pursue a scientific career.

### In Faraday's words:

Faraday was constantly thinking about the world around him in a scientific way, but he also had a great sense of humour. When he wrote to his best friend Benjamin Abbott (from the City Philosophical Society) he was always poking fun at himself: *'I set off from you at a run and did not stop until I found myself in the midst of a puddle and a* **quandary** *of thoughts respecting the heat generated by animal bodies by exercise ... [On falling] ... the* **velocity** *and* **momentum** *of falling bodies next struck not only my mind but my head, my ears, my hands, my back and various other parts of my body ...'*

*Handsome, dynamic and a brilliant lecturer, Humphry Davy immediately converted Michael Faraday to his ideas on electricity.*

# A fortunate fight

By the autumn of 1812, Michael Faraday was very unhappy about the direction his life was taking. Determined to leave bookbinding behind him, he wrote to Sir Joseph Banks, president of the **Royal Society**, begging to be placed in any scientific post, however lowly. But he had no response, and began to despair. In December he wrote to Sir Humphry Davy personally, again begging for a position and sending along the bound copy of notes he had made from Davy's lectures. Davy was flattered – but there were no vacancies.

Then Faraday's first chance came. Davy injured his eye during an explosive experiment, and could neither read nor write. Faraday was invited to spend a few days making fair copies of some of Davy's notes for publication. This brief taste of the scientific life fired Faraday's determination even more.

## A lucky break

In 1813 Michael Faraday was given his second – and full-time – opportunity to join the ranks of the real scientists. A laboratory assistant at the **Royal Institution** became involved in a brawl with the man who made the instruments needed for the experiments. The assistant was dismissed on the spot, and Humphry Davy suggested Michael Faraday as his replacement. He was appointed with a salary of one **guinea** a week, plus two rooms at the Institution, fuel and candles, which gave him the opportunity to move out of the family home.

Sir Joseph Banks was president of the Royal Society at the time when Faraday was struggling to find his first scientific post.

## Sir Humphry Davy

Humphry Davy was one of the great scientists of his day. He was born in Cornwall in 1778 and, after an early **apprenticeship** to a surgeon and **apothecary**, he became deeply involved in chemistry. By the time he was 23, he was assistant lecturer in chemistry and director of the laboratory at the Royal Institution, and a year later gained the professorship of chemistry. He was a very active researcher and always liked to see a practical application for his discoveries. He carried out enormous amounts of work on **electrochemistry**, was a **fellow of the Royal Society** at the age of 25 and by 32 was regarded as the best chemist of his time. Faraday was fortunate indeed to come to the attention of such a brilliant and influential man.

*Michael Faraday was full of enthusiasm for science and for life when, as a young man, he started work at the Royal Institution.*

### In Davy's words:

Davy recommended the young man he had met briefly as follows: *'His name is Michael Faraday. His habits seem good, his disposition is active and cheerful, and his manner intelligent.'*

# The trip to Europe

*Dark grey metallic crystals that produced a beautiful purple gas when heated – this was the strange new substance, extracted from sea algae, that the French showed Davy and his companions. Davy named it iodine.*

Faraday was delighted with his new job and threw himself into it, body and soul. Within weeks of starting out as a laboratory assistant he was carrying out his own research, and was soon a valued member of the team at the **Royal Institution**. Then, in the autumn of 1813, Humphry Davy offered him a place on his expedition to Europe, promising that his position at the Institution would still be there when they returned.

## A European experience

Travelling around Europe during the break up of the **Napoleonic Empire** could have been difficult and dangerous, but Davy's reputation was such that doors opened wherever they went. Not only did Faraday benefit from Davy's explanations of the science they experienced as they travelled, he also had the opportunity to meet many of the other great physicists and chemists of the time. In France, eminent scientists met and shared ideas with the party from Britain. The French scientists showed the British a new substance they had discovered.

Davy set to work and very rapidly decided that this substance was a new **element**, similar to **chlorine**. He suggested a name for it – **iodine**. Faraday was fascinated to see the master chemist at work in this way, made copious notes and learnt a great deal about scientific technique along the way.

In 1814 they entered Italy, again talking with the local scientists and taking in all the country had to offer.

## The fly in the ointment

Faraday's enjoyment of his European trip was spoiled by just one thing – Humphry Davy's wife. Lady Davy was a chatterbox and a snob, not a very thoughtful or pleasant woman. She picked on Faraday with her sharp tongue, perhaps because he was so close to her husband. At first it simply made him homesick and unhappy, but later he began to retaliate as he decided he would no longer suffer her insults in silence. Humphry Davy himself was caught in the middle! The unpleasant atmosphere, combined with the escape of Napoleon from exile on the island of Elba, led the company to cut short their visit and in spring 1815 they hastily returned to England.

*Florence was the city which really captivated Michael Faraday. He loved the climate, the architecture and the scientific wonders such as Galileo's telescope.*

# A job at the Royal Institution

Back in England, Michael Faraday returned to the **Royal Institution**, no longer a lowly laboratory assistant but now with the title Assistant and Superintendent of the **Apparatus** of the Laboratory and Mineralogical Collection, earning the princely sum of 30 shillings (£1.50) a week. He was also given some better rooms at the very top of the Royal Institution, but only after a battle with the current occupant who did not want to give them up! Faraday had to work very hard to evict the man living in the rooms, but he was determined to move in and eventually succeeded.

## A focus on work

Faraday took his work very seriously. As well as working on research projects, he spent much time in the library, building up his knowledge and understanding of chemistry. In 1816 he published his first paper and also began to spread his knowledge by delivering lectures. However, he was a very modest man and

*Hans Christian Oersted was a Danish scientist who spent his life working on the links between electricity and magnetism.*

### HANS CHRISTIAN OERSTED

While working at the University of Copenhagen, Oersted (1777–1851) discovered that if a compass needle was brought near to a wire that had an electric current flowing through it, the needle was affected and moved. He also found that the magnetic force created by the current was circular, surrounding the wire. In 1820 he published a paper describing his findings, and it was this that triggered Michael Faraday into changing the focus of his research.

took the trouble to study lecturing techniques and styles before he began to give talks himself. Between the years 1815 and 1819 he gave lectures to the City Philosophical Society, the very group amongst whom he himself had first heard Mr Tatum's lectures and been inspired. Faraday was increasingly known as a competent chemist and people turned to him as a consultant for advice on their research. But in 1821 Faraday moved away from his beloved chemistry to try his hand at investigating **electromagnetism**.

*Faraday's electromagnetic apparatus. This was the first electric motor.*

## A new direction

Oersted's discoveries (see panel) stimulated scientists – or natural philosophers as they still liked to be known – all over Europe. Davy immediately began working on the discoveries, but in his haste jumped to the wrong conclusions. He then teamed up with his great friend and fellow scientist William Wollaston, who developed an idea that a wire could be made to revolve around its own **axis**. He and Davy could not make this work, and discussed the difficulties with Faraday. Faraday was busy with other things at the time, but not long afterwards, in 1821, he felt he could see a solution to the problem Davy and Wollaston had posed. He produced, with great ingenuity, the first-ever electric motor with a wire rotating around a magnet.

# Controversy!

*This is William Hyde Wollaston. A misunderstanding with Wollaston was the cause of much distress to Faraday.*

When Michael Faraday first set up his electric motor in 1821, he realized how much it would interest William Wollaston. He visited Wollaston's house in the hope of discussing these new ideas with him, but he was away. Instead of waiting until Wollaston returned, Faraday was so excited by his discovery that he went ahead and published his results, a decision he was to regret for a long time to come. Immediately, everyone who had known Wollaston's ideas on rotations in a magnetic field leapt to the conclusion that Faraday had stolen these ideas, added a bit to them and then published a paper about them, without any acknowledgement of the help he had received from either Wollaston himself or from Humphry Davy.

## Shamed!

Michael Faraday was deeply embarrassed and shamed by the outcry that his publication on **electromagnetism** caused. He tried very hard to explain his actions to Wollaston, who was much his senior, but Wollaston took little notice. Davy also made little effort to help his young assistant – he too seems to have felt resentment towards Faraday and maybe a little jealous of his success. Relations within the **Royal Institution** became very strained, until in 1823 Faraday apologized again to both Davy and Wollaston and returned to his chemistry. For the following six years he spent most of his time investigating and developing types of steel that would not rust.

## Chlorine chemistry

Faraday had always been fascinated by **chlorine**, a yellowy-green poisonous gas, and in the 1820s he carried out some new investigations into the **element**. In 1823 he prepared some chlorine hydrate (chlorine combined chemically with hydrogen and oxygen) and, at Davy's suggestion, heated it in a sealed tube. He first thought that the oily yellow liquid that collected was dirt from the tube – but then realized it was liquid chlorine. Faraday went on to liquefy a number of other substances, including sulphur dioxide, carbon dioxide and ammonia. These are not easy procedures, and a number of times the sealed tubes exploded, causing damage – fortunately temporary – to his eyes. But now Faraday created controversy once more. When he published the results of his experiments with liquefied chlorine he made a brief mention of Sir Humphry Davy. However, Sir Humphry felt he had not been given sufficient prominence and once again Faraday fell from grace.

**In Faraday's words:**

Less than a week after the publication of his paper, Faraday wrote to his friend James Stodart: *'You know perfectly well what distress the unexpected reception of my paper on magnetism in public has caused me, and you will not therefore be surprised at my anxiety to get out of it ...'*

*When Faraday liquefied poisonous yellow chlorine, he again ran into difficulties, this time with Sir Humphry Davy.*

# Faraday and his faith

One of the most important factors in the life of Michael Faraday was his deep and abiding faith in the teachings of the **Sandemanian** Church. The Sandemanians were a small and exclusive religious group, or sect, that had appeared originally as a breakaway group from the Church of Scotland. Robert Sandeman, from whom the sect took its name, was the son-in-law of one of the original founders, John Glas. It was Sandeman who wrote down the teachings of the new Church, based wholly on the teachings of Jesus Christ in the New Testament.

Sandemanians followed a number of principles, and Faraday stuck closely to these throughout his life. In memory of Jesus Christ's sacrifice for people, the love-feast (a 'Last Supper' type of meal) and the washing of each other's feet were important rituals. Christ's kingdom is not of this world, and so members of the Church were discouraged from becoming wealthy and worldly. Sandemanians tried to live in imitation of the way Christ lived, but in this they made themselves exclusive and somewhat isolated. True friendships and marriages were only allowed among their own small community.

*Faraday's work would have been impossible without Alessandro Volta, the man who invented the battery in about 1800. Here he demonstrates his invention to Napoleon.*

## A change of heart

Michael Faraday was so dedicated to his work and the search for scientific truth that he had no time for thoughts of women or marriage.

One of Faraday's Sandemanian friends, Edward Barnard, gleefully told his sister Sarah about an anti-love poem Faraday had written. Whether she took this as a challenge we shall never know, but she very rapidly made a great impression on Faraday. Michael was a good-looking and successful young man. Sarah was a warm, charming and attractive young woman. It was not long before Faraday was pursuing her with all the energy he had previously given to his work. Fortunately, both Sarah and her family liked Michael – indeed Sarah's feelings went well beyond mere liking! On 12 June 1821, Sarah Barnard and Michael Faraday were married. Theirs was a partnership of deep love and affection that was to last throughout their lives.

> **In Faraday's words:**
>
> Faraday penned some lines about marriage:
>
> *'What is the pest and plague of human life?*
>
> *And what is the curse that often brings a wife?*
>
> *'tis Love.'*

*Sarah Barnard (seen here in later years) became Sarah Faraday, and changed Faraday's views on love and marriage for ever.*

# An important man

*Davy, inventor of the miner's safety lamp (shown here), was certainly unhappy at the prospect of Faraday becoming a fellow of the Royal Society.*

By 1823, when he was still only 32, Michael Faraday had accumulated an impressive body of work. His discovery of the electric motor alone had made him an international figure, as people in many countries recognized its potential and began developing motors that could be used in different ways. However, Faraday himself showed little interest in the practical applications of his work. His patient, meticulous approach to his research marked him out as a true laboratory-based scientist of the highest quality. In 1823, in recognition of his work, he was proposed for election as a **fellow of the Royal Society**. Then, as now, this was the greatest honour that could be given to a living scientist in Great Britain. But Faraday knew that the issue of Wollaston and the electric motor still rankled with Sir Humphry Davy, president of the **Royal Society**. As Faraday's star was rising, so Davy's was beginning to fade. In fact Davy was probably jealous of the impact Faraday was making.

In 1824 Michael Faraday was duly elected a fellow of the Royal Society – with only one person opposing the election!

*This is the Royal Institution, where Michael Faraday carried out much of his greatest work and to which he was deeply dedicated.*

## The Royal Institution

Davy was too honest a man to hold a grudge against the genius of Faraday for long. As the older man's health began to deteriorate, he spent less and less time at his research in the **Royal Institution**. In 1825 Davy suggested that Faraday should be appointed director of the laboratory at the Royal Institution. This change of heart took Faraday by surprise, but he did not let Davy down. He was delighted with his new position – even though it brought him no more money – and he carried it out with unswerving dedication. He and Sarah lived in rooms at the Royal Institution, so Faraday could work late in his laboratory but still see his wife. Their family parties and celebrations became well known, and young nephews and nieces were frequent visitors to the laboratories, where they watched the great scientist and his colleagues at work.

### In Faraday's words:

Years after the event, Faraday described an interview he had with Davy about the certificate which indicated his standing for election to the Royal Society: *'Sir H. Davy told me I must take down my certificate. I replied … it was put up by my proposers. He then said I must get my proposers to take it down … Then he said "I as president will take it down …"'*

# Faraday's functions

Michael Faraday had a gift for explaining the science he loved so dearly. The lecture theatre was always packed to capacity – even Prince Albert and the Prince of Wales attended the Christmas lectures.

**In Lady Holland's words:**

Lady Holland, who attended some of Faraday's lectures, described the flavour of the evening: '... *he had his audience at his command ... he had nothing to fret him and could give his eloquence full sway. [His] ... eloquence compelled attention and insisted on sympathy. It waked the young from their visions and the old from their dreams. His enthusiasm sometimes carried him to the point of ecstasy ... his hair streamed out from his head, his hands were full of nervous action, his light, lithe body seemed to quiver with its eager life. His audience took fire with him.'* Clearly, Faraday was a hugely inspirational speaker!

When Michael Faraday became director of the laboratory, he brought a breath of fresh air to the **Royal Institution**. Davy had been a brilliant lecturer in his prime, and Faraday had worked hard to be a worthy successor. One of the first things he did as director was to invite members to visit the Royal Institution on certain evenings to hear of the latest research and discoveries that the scientists were making. By 1826 these meetings had been moved to a regular slot on Friday evenings during winter and spring. These Friday evening discourses soon became famous. Faraday's idea was to try and share with ordinary people the beauty, charm and usefulness of science – an aim which is still important today. At the same time the lectures raised much needed income for the Royal Institution, as people willingly paid to come and listen to great scientists speaking about their work. Faraday himself gave over a hundred of these 'discourses' during his time at the Royal Institution.

## The children's champion

Faraday felt that young people as well as adults should have the opportunity to hear about exciting science at first hand, and so he introduced his famous Christmas lectures for children. These lectures brought out the very best in Faraday, as his own enthusiasm was reflected and magnified by that of his young audience. He once famously threw the coal scuttle, fire tongs and poker at the great electromagnet of the Royal Institution – and all these heavy objects flew through the air and stuck to it!

## Into the future

The Christmas lectures for young people that Faraday introduced, and for many years delivered, are still thriving today. Every year, one of the foremost scientists of the day runs a course of six lectures that are given live and also televised.

*Through the medium of television, the excitement and wonder of science can reach not hundreds but millions of children each year. Michael Faraday would be delighted to see his Christmas lectures still going strong.*

# The work goes on

As Michael Faraday settled into his post as director of the laboratory at the **Royal Institution**, he found many other offers of jobs came his way. He was so widely respected for his work, and admired both personally and as a lecturer and teacher, that many other institutions tried to persuade him to work for them. One of the most notable offers came around 1827, from the newly formed University of London. They offered him the professorship of chemistry, with the freedom to build up the department of chemistry as he wished. But Faraday turned this offer down, as he did almost all others. He said that he was so grateful to the Royal Institution for the help and support it had given him early in his career, that he wished to remain there now he had become famous, and do all he could to further its interests.

## Research, research ...

Faraday still spent most of his time doing active research. Fascinated by everything and anything, he would set himself questions to answer, and conduct rigorous experiments. For example, some of the richer London homes were lit by gas made from coal and oils, such as whale oil, supplied in compressed form in special cylinders. Intrigued by the liquid residue left in the cylinders when they were empty of gas, Faraday set out to investigate the liquid, separating it out, purifying and analysing it. One component had not been seen before, and Faraday called it 'bicarburet of hydrogen'. This important **organic** chemical is now well known as benzene.

*A whale is an unlikely source of benzene! But the gas that Michael Faraday investigated, and that led him to the discovery of benzene, was formed by heating whale oil and storing the gas given off under pressure.*

Faraday was also involved – not very successfully – in some experiments to try and develop glass that would be particularly good for making lenses. But increasingly his mind was turning again towards electricity and **electromagnetism**, and gradually his other research was laid aside.

## Personal sadness

In these years of professional development, Michael and Sarah Faraday had to deal with one great personal sadness. It became increasingly apparent that they were not going to be able to have children of their own. Both of them loved the company of children and young people, so this must have been a bitter blow to come to terms with. Sarah poured much of her maternal feeling into caring for her absent-minded husband, and they both played a major part in their wider families, with various nieces spending much of their childhood with their beloved uncle and aunt.

Faraday's simple apparatus was described in detail in his pages of carefully made notes.

Over the years, Faraday repeated the electrical and magnetic experiments performed by Oersted, Ampère and others. He became convinced that as electricity could produce magnetic effects, there must be a way to use magnetism to produce electricity. He became so determined to solve this problem that it became almost an obsession with him. Legend has it that he would always carry a small iron bar and a coil of wire in his pocket, so that if he had a spare moment he could fiddle around and try to work out a solution.

## The iron ring

Faraday made a soft iron ring and wound coil after coil of copper wire around it. He connected it to a **galvanometer** (which would measure any current that flowed) and then pushed a bar magnet into the ring. A current was set up as the magnet moved into the ring, and again as it moved out – but nothing happened while it was in the middle.

## Making electricity

Finally, after days of frantic work, Faraday made his breakthrough. If pulsating currents could be made by pushing a magnet in and out of a **helix** of wire, would it be possible to create a steady current by using a constantly rotating movement? Faraday set up an **apparatus** where a copper disc was rotated between the poles of a magnet, and contacts on the edge of the wheel led any current generated to the galvanometer. To his dismay, when the wheel turned, the galvanometer did not move. Faraday tried numerous arrangements of the leads until finally, by connecting one to the edge of the disc and one to the centre, he recorded a weak but continuous deflection of the galvanometer. The deflection became larger as the wheel turned faster.

In two months of unbelievably intensive work, Michael Faraday had developed the **dynamo**! His discovery was to make the generation of electricity possible all over the world and change society for ever. But Faraday was never very interested in the practical applications of his work. He published his first results in 1831 and then, utterly exhausted by his efforts, he and Sarah took a well-earned break.

*The iron ring on which Faraday experimented to discover a way of using magnetism to generate electricity.*

*The American Joseph Henry was the scientist who really pipped Faraday at the post with his work on the use of magnetism to generate electricity.*

Michael Faraday was, first and foremost, a **theoretical** scientist. This means he carried out his research and worked on his ideas for the pleasure of understanding how things worked. Once a problem was solved, he had little real interest in how the science he had discovered might be applied in everyday life. However, on the other side of the Atlantic, another inspired young scientist was working in the same area of electricity and magnetism – and he was of a much more practical frame of mind.

## Joseph Henry

Joseph Henry (1797–1878) was born and raised in Albany, New York, where he studied and gained his first professorship in 1826. He was appointed professor of natural philosophy at the College of New Jersey (now Princeton University) in 1832. Like Faraday he was fascinated by the relationship between electricity and magnetism, and developed the most powerful electromagnets of his time. This work of Henry's almost certainly affected Faraday's thinking. Henry actually discovered the principle of **electromagnetic induction** several months before Faraday produced his first **dynamo**. But – also like Faraday – Henry had been criticized for using other people's ideas. Still hurt by this criticism, Henry held back from publishing any more results, giving Faraday the time to reach the same conclusions and make his findings public. Thus, it is Faraday who is usually credited with the discovery of electromagnetic induction and the dynamo rather than his American counterpart.

*The telegraph meant that news, information about weather conditions and cries for help could all be sent and received far faster than ever before. This changed the face of society.*

## Theory and practice

The differences between the two men became very obvious as their careers progressed. Faraday continued to investigate the theoretical basis of physics, while Henry became very involved in the practical applications of what he had discovered. He greatly increased the lifting power and efficiency of electromagnets, making them useful in industry. He designed a new and better electric motor, and, most importantly, in 1831 he developed the first **telegraph** system using **electromagnetism**. This led eventually to the invention of the telephone. At the beginning of the 19th century, messages took days or weeks to cross a country or continent. By the end of the century, the same messages could be sent almost instantaneously by telegraph.

In 1846 Henry was elected secretary of the newly formed Smithsonian Institute and in this role he set up research efforts in many areas of science. He was the first to organize **meteorological studies** and to use the telegraph to transmit daily weather reports – work that led to the formation of the United States Weather Bureau. Henry used his mind in a very different way from Faraday, producing practical solutions to problems. Both were great men however, and extraordinary thinkers for their time.

31

# Faraday's laws

Around 1820 a major controversy broke out. It had been noticed that if an electric current flowed through water, two gases – hydrogen and oxygen – were produced. This observation caused mayhem. Theories abounded among the great scientists of the day, but none stood up to testing and none of them was right! In 1832 Michael Faraday entered the arena and began to apply his mind to the observations that had been made. He worked by passing electricity through acidified water. The conclusions he had reached by 1833 completely revolutionized the way **electrolysis** was understood, and built the foundations for all our modern understanding of the science.

## Electrolysis

In electrolysis, electricity passes through a solution of water and a substance called an **electrolyte**, or through a molten material. Tiny particles carrying different charges are attracted to either the positive or the negative **electrode**. At these electrodes they either lose or gain **electrons** to form stable **atoms** or **molecules**.

Not only did Michael Faraday explain what was happening during electrolysis, he also introduced the terminology – electrolysis, electrolyte, electrode – that we still use today.

*Faraday's understanding of electrolysis shed light on a subject that was puzzling many of the great minds of the day.*

*A worker in the modern electrolysis industry. Today electrolysis provides us not only with useful objects such as aluminium foil, but also with things simply to enjoy such as silver- and gold-plated jewellery.*

## Faraday's laws

As part of his careful work on electrolysis Faraday measured the amounts of different substances given off during the process. As a result of all his observations and measurements he formulated two laws that can be used to predict the outcome of any type of electrolysis. They are known as Faraday's laws and they are still in use.

## Into the future

Electrolysis is a common process in industry today. Aluminium, one of the most widely used metals, is extracted from its ore by electrolysis, and so are fluorine and sodium. Copper is refined by electrolysis, and brine is split to form sodium hydroxide, chlorine and hydrogen. Processes such as plating with silver, gold or copper all use the same method of electrolysis. The calculations needed for all these processes still rely on Faraday's laws.

### In Faraday's words:

Faraday's first law states: *'The quantity of a substance deposited, evolved or dissolved at an electrode during electrolysis is directly proportional to the quantity of electricity passed through the electrolyte.'*

Faraday's second law states: *'The quantities of different substances deposited, evolved or dissolved at electrodes by the passage of the same quantity of electricity are directly proportional to the combining weights of the substances.'*

# Illness strikes

In 1831 Faraday gave up much of his well-paid consulting work because he was determined to focus his energies on his work with **electrolysis**. This meant he was about £800 a year poorer, a sum of money that had a marked effect on the standard of living that he and Sarah could enjoy. As **Sandemanians** they gave little thought to this, but friends and colleagues felt strongly that the government should award him a pension in recognition of his work. In 1835 this pension was finally granted and accepted. However, at around the same time and after several years of very concentrated work, Michael's health let him down suddenly and dramatically.

## The end of a career?

The first sign that something was wrong was when Faraday began to suffer giddy spells and, even more frighteningly, complete lapses of memory. He had to cut down his work time more and more, until eventually he reluctantly listened to his doctors and took a complete nine-month break with Sarah in Switzerland.

When Faraday returned to England, he did no more work at all for four years, and then began to do research again only at a very slow pace.

In 1840, while his health was still fragile, Faraday was made an elder of the Sandemanian Church, which involved giving sermons, carrying out services and supporting other members of the Church community. Sarah and Michael Faraday were well known for their open-heartedness and generosity to their friends, their family and their Church. But at the same time there were troubles in the Church to do with the way of interpreting the teachings, which Faraday found very stressful. The disagreements ended on 31 March 1844 with Faraday, his brother, sister, father-in-law and about fifteen other Sandemanians being excluded from the Church. This brought Faraday to a very low point indeed, but when he was restored to the fellowship five weeks later he picked himself up and began a remarkable recovery.

*Much of Faraday's recovery, and his continued ability to work, was the result of the devoted care and protection given to him by his beloved wife Sarah.*

## Back in harness

From 1845 onwards Faraday's health recovered almost miraculously, to the point where he could once again immerse himself in his beloved science. Another seventeen years of brilliant research were to emerge from his laboratory, although his memory was never again as good. He wrote himself copious notes to make sure he could remember what he was doing, making it possible for him to continue as a respected and successful scientist.

During the 1850s Michael Faraday continued to work. He was offered many honours during these later years, including presidency of the **Royal Society** twice. He was offered it once, refused and then was later asked again, but he still refused. He was also offered a knighthood, but he turned all these honours down because they did not fit with the beliefs of his **Sandemanian** faith.

## The memory fades

It became increasingly obvious that Faraday's glory days were over. His memory, which had given him trouble for years, was frequently letting him down. Although Faraday had regained his physical strength after his earlier illness, his mind, and particularly his memory, were never the same again. He could remember the past but not the present. He dared not work in the same areas of research as other people because he could not remember what they had done and feared he might again appear to steal ideas.

A group of Royal Society members visited Faraday (second from left) in 1858, inviting him to become president. He refused because of his religious beliefs.

In 1861 Faraday retired, with great sadness, from his post as lecturer at his beloved **Royal Institution**, although he remained superintendent of the laboratories. In 1864 he gave up his role as an elder of the Sandemanian Church and finally, in 1865, he retired from all his remaining posts. He and Sarah moved from the Royal Institution to a house in Hampton Court, provided by Queen Victoria herself in recognition of his achievements.

## Fading light

From 1865 onwards Faraday deteriorated rapidly. Towards the end of his life he was rarely lucid and was unable to do anything for himself, spending most of his time sitting in a chair staring vacantly into space. He was cared for lovingly by the ever-devoted Sarah and their nieces. Finally, on 25 August 1867, Michael Faraday died, still sitting quietly in his chair – although all that had made him one of the great scientists had been lost, long before his heart ceased to beat.

Faraday's funeral was in keeping with his Sandemanian faith. Not for him the pomp and ceremony of a burial in Westminster Abbey. Michael Faraday was laid to rest in Highgate Cemetery after a very private and plain ceremony, and his headstone simply reads:

Michael Faraday    Born 22 September 1791
Died 25 August 1867

**In Faraday's words:**

*'My memory wearies me greatly in working; for I cannot remember from day to day the conclusions I came to ... I do not remember the order of things or even the facts themselves.'*

# Focus on Faraday

*Faraday spent his scientific life almost entirely at the **Royal Institution**. It has preserved much of his original apparatus and notes as a tribute to one of its most famous members.*

Michael Faraday was a scientist whose work spanned a great variety of disciplines. He made enormous contributions to chemistry, to the study of **electromagnetism**, to the understanding of the nature of electricity and to **electrochemistry**. His work led later to the development of an area of physics known as **field theory**. His work covered light, gravity, glass and steel along the way.

## Faraday the genius

The impact of Michael Faraday's work was recognized and honoured by his peers in his own lifetime. Not for him the struggle to make ends meet, battling against hostile fellow workers. He made a living from his science right from the beginning, and earned enough throughout his life to live the way he chose. Fellow scientists respected and admired his work, even if at times the admiration was tinged with envy. Faraday had a remarkable gift of focus – he would wait until a problem had baffled many of his peers and then apply himself to it with obsessional vigour until he came up with the solution. It must have been galling at times to be one of the many others who came close, but lost out to Faraday's genius. He was even awarded the ultimate accolade – he had a unit of electrical current named after him. The amount of electricity needed to release approximately one **mole** of any substance at an **electrode** is a **faraday**.

## Faraday the educator

Faraday made his mark on the society in which he lived in another way too. More than anyone else before him he worked to encourage the public understanding of science. His Friday evening discourses and the Christmas lectures for young people had an enormous impact during his lifetime, and continue to do so long after his death. There are few scientists who have done so much to involve and interest other people in the subject that they study.

*Michael Faraday loved to think about problems just for the pleasure of solving them, not for their usefulness. His work has helped us find out about many areas of **theoretical** physics, of which this lightning is a beautiful example.*

## Faraday the theoretician

Another way in which Faraday differed from at least some of his contemporaries was in his attitude to his scientific work. He was interested in science for science's sake. He wanted to find out the answers to the questions that arose in his head for their own sake, so that he and others should better understand the beauty and order of the natural world. He had little interest in using the discoveries he made in a practical way – he left the applications to others.

# Faraday's legacy

*Whatever the amount, wherever the place, the generation of electricity depends on the dynamo developed by Michael Faraday.*

The work of Michael Faraday is fundamental to our modern understanding of electricity and magnetism. It has had an enormous effect on the modern world in a variety of ways. Perhaps one of the most important aspects of everyday life that is based on the theories of Michael Faraday is the generation (production) of electricity. It does not matter whether the energy source for a power station is coal, oil, gas or nuclear fuel, when it comes to generating electricity the process depends on a **dynamo**. This is also true for wind power and wave power, however big or small the **generator**, or wherever in the world it is being used. Without the dynamo the world would be a very different place. And while American scientist Joseph Henry and others developed the practical applications of the dynamo, it was Faraday who explored deeply into the theory of how and why it works.

## A glimpse into the unknown

Modern particle physics is an area of academic study beyond the understanding of many of us. However, the **theoretical** exploration of the very nature of the matter that makes up our universe could yet yield secrets that will have enormous benefit for the human race. This branch of physics has its roots directly in the work that Faraday carried out on **field theory**.

*Magnetic resonance imaging – part of the legacy of Michael Faraday which is having a major impact on the health of people today. This scan shows the thorax and abdomen of a woman.*

A much more practical legacy of Faraday's work is the use of magnetic resonance imaging (MRI) in the diagnosis of diseases such as cancer. This technique has moved Faraday's detailed work on magnetism and electricity right into the 21st century. It gives doctors a way of seeing clearly into the body without opening it up or damaging it in any way. X-rays were the first scientific tool that allowed us to do this, but their uses are limited. MRI scans of parts of the body give doctors sharp detail of all the different tissues, and make the task of finding cancer in the body much easier. More than that, they make it possible to see precisely the extent of a tumour, making surgery and treatment increasingly accurate – and therefore much more effective. Faraday's legacy of scientific discovery will last for the foreseeable future, and appear in many different areas of our lives. His was a rare talent.

# A man to remember

A British stamp, produced in 1991. This is a true testament to Faraday's great and lasting legacy.

Michael Faraday began his life in the humble home of a **blacksmith**. He was raised in a family short of money but strong in the faith of their own **Sandemanian** Church. By the time he died he was a figure of international renown, respected for his work in many areas of science, a man who had made his mark, not only on the age in which he lived but on generations to come.

## A life of dedication

Michael Faraday's first job was as an **apprentice** bookbinder. He did not continue with this career, but it gave him the opportunity to move into science.

From Faraday's arrival at the **Royal Institution** his working life was dedicated to the pursuit of scientific knowledge. It is astonishing that one man could work on so many areas of chemistry and physics with such success. Faraday identified new **elements**, worked on stainless steel and optical glass, and made major breakthroughs in our understanding of electricity and **electromagnetism**. He discovered the principles of the first electric motor and the **dynamo** (fundamental to the generation of electricity). He unravelled the mysteries of **electrolysis**, determined the strength of current at the **electrodes** and made the first steps into **field theory**. On top of this, he ran the Royal Institution and set up both the Friday evening discourses and the Christmas lectures for young people. It is not overstating the case to say that Faraday was a man of genius.

## Personal loyalties

In his private life Michael Faraday was just as dedicated as in his working life. His private dedication was to his beloved wife, Sarah, his family and his Church. Sarah and Michael were close partners all through their marriage, and although they were denied the joy of their own children they took great delight in their nieces and nephews, and played a large part in these young people's lives. And to the Sandemanian Church – demanding, challenging and exclusive – Michael Faraday gave total loyalty, even though at times the conflict between his work and the fame that came his way, and the beliefs of his Church community must have been very hard to deal with.

At the end of Faraday's life came the great sadness of his decline into senility. It distressed his wife and family to see his struggle to remember the simplest things. What is hardest is to think of how Faraday himself felt, when he was long aware of, and frustrated by, the deterioration of his mental powers. But nothing that occurred at the end of his life could dim the brilliance of the legacy he left behind – a legacy that still affects all our lives today.

*Once Michael Faraday was given his first chance at the Royal Institution by the great Sir Humphry Davy, he never looked back.*

# Timeline

| | |
|---|---|
| **1698** | A steam-powered pump was invented for use in mines. |
| **1770** | A steam-powered carriage was invented to pull artillery – heavy guns used for fighting on land. It was not successful as it was so difficult to steer. |
| **1782** | James Watt designed a steam system that would produce rotary movement. |
| **1791** | Michael Faraday born 22 September. |
| **1800** | Alessandro Volta demonstrates the first battery. |
| **1805** | Michael is taken on as an **apprentice** bookbinder. |
| **1812** | Attends lectures given by the great scientist Sir Humphry Davy and vows to pursue a scientific career. |
| **1813** | Appointed laboratory assistant at the **Royal Institution** and later accompanies Davy on an expedition to Europe. |
| **1815** | Napoleon escapes from exile on the island of Elba. |
| **1816** | Michael publishes his first paper and gives lectures on chemistry to the City Philosophical Society. |
| **1820** | Hans Christian Oersted publishes a paper on **electromagnetism**. |
| **1821** | Michael produces the first electric motor and marries Sarah Barnard. |
| **1823** | Publishes the results of his experiments with liquid **chlorine** and upsets Humphry Davy. |
| **1824** | Elected a **fellow of the Royal Society**. |
| **1825** | Davy forgives Michael who is then appointed director of the laboratory at the Royal Institution. |
| **1826** | Michael's Friday evening discourses at the Royal Institution become hugely popular. |
| **1831** | Invents the **dynamo**. |
| **1833** | Faraday's laws on **electrolysis** are formulated. |
| **1835** | Receives a pension but his health begins to fail. |
| **1840** | Made an elder of the **Sandemanian** Church. |
| **1844** | Troubles in the Church cause Michael's exclusion and take a further toll on his health. |
| **1845** | Michael is restored to the Church and recovers his health. |
| **1858** | The **Royal Society** asks Michael to be its president but he refuses on religious grounds. |

| 1865 | His mind failing, Michael is unable to work any longer. He retires and moves to Hampton Court. |
| 1867 | Michael Faraday dies on 25 August, aged 75. |

# Places to visit and further reading

## Places to visit

The Science Museum, South Kensington, London – houses displays on electricity and magnetism. You can visit the museum on the Internet at www.nmsi.ac.uk

The Royal Institution, Albermarle Street, London – the Institution's museum includes a large number of Faraday's original instruments and a recreation of what his laboratory would have looked like. Visit the museum online at www.ri.ac.uk

A power station – there are many around the country that are open for visits

## Further reading

Good, Keith: *Exciting Electrics* (Evans Brothers, London, 1999)

Langley, Andrew: *Victorian Britain* – History of Britain series (Heinemann Library, Oxford, 1997)

Langley, Andrew: *Georgian Britain* – History of Britain series (Heinemann Library, Oxford, 1994)

Oxlade, Chris: *Electricity and Magnetism* – Science Topics series (Heinemann Library, Oxford, 1999)

# Glossary

**alchemy** ancient 'science' which aimed at understanding matter in order to turn base metals into gold, and finding the secret of eternal life

**apothecary** old name for a pharmacist

**apparatus** set of instruments for a particular task

**apprentice(ship)** someone bound (the act of being bound) to an employer for a set length of time to learn a trade or craft

**atom** smallest particle of an element

**axis** line around which a rotating body turns

**blacksmith** someone who works with iron, shoeing horses, making railings and so on

**chlorine** gaseous element

**dynamo** machine for converting mechanical energy into electrical energy by the rotation of copper wire coils in a magnetic field

**electrochemistry** study of the links between electricity and chemistry

**electrode** conductor through which an electric current enters or leaves a cell (battery)

**electrolysis** breaking down of a chemical compound using electricity

**electrolyte** substance that conducts electricity when it is in solution or melted

**electromagnetic induction** production of an electric current using a magnetic field

**electromagnetism** magnetic field produced by an electric current

**electrons** tiny negative particles that make up part of the structure of an atom

**element** substance made up of only one type of atom

**faraday** amount of electricity needed to release one mole of any substance at an electrode

**fellow(ship) of the Royal Society** member (the state of being a member) of the Royal Society. Membership is by invitation only, and it is awarded to people who have made an outstanding contribution to science.

**field theory** theory explaining the way in which objects not in contact can influence each other

**French Revolution** revolution that occurred in France when the monarchy was replaced by a republic

**galvanometer** device used to detect or measure very small electric currents

**generator** machine for making electrical energy from mechanical energy; generators burn fuel, or use the power of water, nuclear, wind or solar energy

**guinea** 21 shillings (£1.05)

**helix** a spiral

**indelible** cannot be rubbed out

**iodine** element in the same chemical family as chlorine

**meteorological studies** study of weather and climate

**mole** amount of any substance that contains approximately $6 \times 10^{23}$ particles

**molecule** particle made up of more than one atom joined together

**momentum** mass times velocity

**Napoleonic Empire** French empire ruled by the Emperor Napoleon around 1804–1814. Countries under his rule included Spain, Italy and Germany.

**organic** relating to living organisms such as animals and plants

**quandary** uncertainty

**Royal Institution** scientific body for research and teaching founded in 1799. The building in which the business of the Institution takes place is also known as the Royal Institution.

**Royal Society** most highly regarded learned body in Britain

**Sandemanians** small religious sect named after Robert Sandeman

**smithy** place where a blacksmith works

**telegraph** communications system that works by sending electrical signals in code through wires

**theoretical** dealing with theories – the abstract ideas and principles behind science – rather than practical application

**velocity** measure of the speed and direction of an object

# Index